contents

NZ, Canada, US and UK readers
Please note that Australian cup and spoon
measurements are metric. A quick conversion
guide appears on page 63.

The takeaway barbecued chicken is a *lifesaver for anyone who wants to make an innovative, nourishing and satisfying meal. When time is short, starting with a cooked chicken means you're halfway there. The ability of cooked chicken to adapt to use in soups or salads, wraps or bakes, pies or pastas is nothing short of remarkable, and its basic plainness lends itself perfectly to almost every cuisine – from Italian to Moroccan, from Chinese to Mexican.*

KNOW YOUR SHOP

While takeaway barbecued chicken can be found in virtually every suburb or town, some are more palatable than others… and some "others" can be questionable in terms of hygiene. Make sure you know the shop from which you buy a chicken, and then make sure you yourself take care of it properly from shop to plate.

COOL IT

Most food poisoning is the result of food that has not been properly refrigerated, and occurs more often in summer when temperatures soar. Some food-poisoning bacteria can survive cooking temperatures and, while not numerous enough to be of concern immediately after the chicken is cooked, it's possible they could multiply if the chicken is left unrefrigerated or kept between 5C and 60C for too long.

HOT TO TROT

As a rule of thumb, never buy barbecued chicken if it is anything other than piping hot; this very high temperature will help kill dangerous bacteria. These bacteria cannot survive at very low temperatures either, so buy the chicken just before you head home, keep it as cool as possible en route and refrigerate it, out of the foil-lined bag, as soon as you arrive. The chicken can be refrigerated while still warm: cut it into sections or remove the meat from the bones before refrigerating it, covered, in a glass bowl, until required.

STUFF AND NONSENSE

If the chicken you've bought comes with stuffing, remove all of it from the bird then either discard it or refrigerate it, covered, separate to the rest of the chicken. Don't keep this stuffing or the chicken longer than 24 hours before using it. Unless the recipe calls for it, discard the fatty skin and the carcass (although you can make a little stock by simmering the bones in a small saucepan of boiling water with a little chopped onion, carrot and celery). To reheat any leftover chicken meat, warm it to a temperature of a minimum 70C for at least 2 minutes.

GIVE IT THE CHOP

When chopping, dicing or slicing the barbecued chicken meat (or home-cooked leftover roast chicken), use a clean knife and chopping board. Never chop cooked chicken on the same board that you use to chop raw meat, seafood or other poultry.

Finger-licking good!

Tuck into your store-bought barbecued chicken with complete confidence after first reading through these guidelines to good hygiene

BARBECUED CHICKEN WEIGHTS

In this book, each takeaway barbecued chicken we used weighed approximately 900g; when skinned and boned, this results in 3 cups (480g) of shredded meat, or 2½ cups (425g) of coarsely chopped meat.

chicken chilli pizza

Ready-made pizza bases are available in all supermarkets and fresh ones can be found at some bakeries.

4 x 125g pizza bases
2 tablespoons tomato paste
1 tablespoon barbecue sauce
1½ teaspoons sambal oelek
1 clove garlic, crushed
1 cup (170g) coarsely chopped cooked chicken
100g button mushrooms, sliced thickly
1 small tomato (130g), halved, sliced thinly
1½ cups (150g) grated pizza cheese
2 teaspoons fresh thyme leaves

Preheat oven to hot.
Place pizza bases on oven tray. Combine paste, sauce, sambal and garlic in small bowl; spread evenly over bases.
Divide chicken, mushroom, tomato and cheese among bases.
Cook, uncovered, in hot oven about 20 minutes or until pizza bases are crisp. Top with thyme.

serves 4
per serving 16.4g fat; 2394kJ (573 cal)
tip Pizza cheese is a convenient blend of coarsely grated processed cheddar, mozzarella and parmesan cheeses available from your supermarket.

chicken wraps

1 large tomato (220g), chopped coarsely
1 medium avocado (320g), chopped coarsely
1 small red onion (100g), chopped coarsely
2 tablespoons coarsely chopped fresh coriander
½ cup (130g) bottled medium chunky salsa
3 cups (480g) shredded cooked chicken
8 large flour tortillas

Combine tomato, avocado, onion, coriander, salsa and chicken in large bowl.
Heat one tortilla in microwave on HIGH (100%) about 20 seconds or until just flexible.
Top tortilla with about an eighth of the chicken filling; roll to enclose filling. Repeat with remaining tortillas and chicken filling.

serves 4
per serving 26.7g fat; 2308kJ (552 cal)
tip Store any remaining uncooked tortillas, sealed tightly, in the refrigerator or freezer.
serving suggestion Tie each wrap with the top end of a green onion, made pliable by soaking it briefly in hot water. This recipe is best assembled close to serving.

chicken lavash rolls

*Tzatziki is a yogurt, cucumber and garlic dip available
from most supermarkets and delicatessens.*

1 cup (170g) coarsely chopped cooked chicken
1½ cups shredded lettuce
⅔ cup (200g) tzatziki dip
4 pieces lavash bread
greek salad
½ medium cucumber (85g), chopped
1 medium tomato (100g), chopped
25g fetta cheese, chopped
2 tablespoons halved, seeded black olives
2 teaspoons lemon juice
2 teaspoons olive oil

Divide chicken, greek salad, lettuce and tzatziki
among lavash; roll up to enclose filling.
greek salad Combine ingredients in medium bowl.

serves 2
per serving 28.1g fat; 3071kJ (735 cal)
tip This recipe is best assembled close to serving.

chicken and mushroom frittata

1 tablespoon olive oil
3 green onions, chopped finely
200g button mushrooms, sliced thinly
1 medium tomato (190g), chopped finely
2½ cups (425g) coarsely chopped cooked chicken
2 tablespoons coarsely chopped fresh
   flat-leaf parsley
6 eggs, beaten lightly
2 cups (250g) coarsely grated cheddar cheese

Heat oil in large frying pan; cook onion and mushroom, stirring until soft. Add tomato; cook until most of the liquid evaporates.
Stir in chicken and parsley. Pour egg over chicken mixture, sprinkle with cheese; cook over low heat until just set. Place pan under heated grill until cheese melts and frittata is browned lightly.
Cut frittata into wedges to serve.

serves 6
per serving 27.7g fat; 1665kJ (398 cal)
serving suggestion Serve with a crisp salad of mixed leaves.

chicken nachos

1 tablespoon vegetable oil
1 medium brown onion (150g), chopped finely
425g can mexican-style beans, drained
3 cups (480g) shredded cooked chicken
390g jar mild nachos topping sauce
230g packet corn chips
2 cups (220g) grated pizza cheese
1 medium avocado (250g), mashed coarsely
⅔ cup (160g) sour cream

Heat oil in medium frying pan; cook onion, stirring, until softened. Stir in beans, chicken and sauce; bring to a boil. Reduce heat; simmer, uncovered, about 3 minutes or until mixture thickens slightly.

Meanwhile, divide corn chips among four microwave-safe serving dishes; top each with cheese. Microwave, one plate at a time, uncovered, on HIGH (100%) about 1 minute or until cheese has melted.

Top plates of corn chips and cheese with equal amounts of chicken mixture, avocado and sour cream.

serves 4
per serving 67.6g fat; 4359kJ (1043 cal)
tip Pizza cheese is a convenient blend of coarsely grated processed cheddar, mozzarella and parmesan cheeses available from your supermarket.

teriyaki rice paper rolls

1 cup (160g) shredded cooked chicken
1 small carrot (70g), grated coarsely
1 small red capsicum (150g), sliced thinly
100g shiitake mushrooms, sliced thinly
50g snow pea tendrils
2 tablespoons coarsely chopped fresh coriander
2 tablespoons teriyaki sauce
1 tablespoon sweet chilli sauce
12 x 22cm rice paper rounds

Combine chicken, carrot, capsicum,
mushroom, tendrils, coriander and sauces
in large bowl; mix gently.
Place one sheet of rice paper in medium bowl of
warm water until just softened; lift sheet carefully from
water, place on board covered with a tea towel.
Place some of the filling in the centre of sheet;
fold in sides, roll top to bottom to enclose filling.
Repeat with remaining rice paper sheets and filling.

serves 4
per serving 2.6g fat; 791kJ (189 cal)
serving suggestion Serve with sweet chilli sauce
or soy sauce.

chicken tostadas

*Refried beans are sold, canned, in most supermarkets,
as are packaged flour tortillas. Made of pinto beans
that are just parboiled then fried with various seasonings,
refried beans are also known by their Mexican name
of frijoles refritos. You will need to purchase one small
iceberg lettuce for this recipe.*

4 large flour tortillas
½ cup (120g) canned refried beans
½ cup (130g) medium chunky salsa
2½ cups (425g) coarsely chopped cooked chicken
1½ cups (125g) grated cheddar cheese
4 cups (240g) finely shredded iceberg lettuce
2 medium tomatoes (380g), chopped coarsely
3 green onions, sliced thinly
½ cup (120g) light sour cream

Preheat grill to hot.
Place tortillas, in single layer, on oven trays.
Combine beans and salsa in small bowl.
Divide bean mixture among tortillas; top with
chicken and cheese. Place under preheated
grill until cheese melts and tortillas' edges crisp.
Top tostadas with lettuce, tomato, onion and
sour cream to serve.

serves 4
per serving 27.5g fat; 2195kJ (525 cal)
tip Store any unused tortillas, sealed tightly,
in the refrigerator or freezer.

chicken, zucchini and corn soup

20g butter
1 large brown onion (200g), chopped finely
1 clove garlic, crushed
2 medium zucchini (240g), grated coarsely
1 litre (4 cups) chicken stock
420g can creamed corn
2½ cups (425g) coarsely chopped cooked chicken
½ cup (125ml) cream

Melt butter in large saucepan; cook onion and garlic, stirring, until onion softens. Add zucchini; cook, stirring, 1 minute. Add stock; bring to a boil. **Stir** in corn and chicken, reduce heat; simmer, uncovered, until chicken is hot. Stir in cream just before serving.

serves 4
per serving 25.6g fat; 1910kJ (457 cal)

chicken laksa

This spicy Malaysian soup has become so popular that its name has made its way into our everyday language.

250g fresh egg noodles
1 teaspoon peanut oil
¼ cup (75g) laksa paste
3¼ cups (800ml) light coconut milk
1 litre (4 cups) chicken stock
2 tablespoons lime juice
1 tablespoon sugar
1 tablespoon fish sauce
6 kaffir lime leaves, torn
2½ cups (425g) coarsely chopped cooked chicken
1 cup (80g) bean sprouts
½ cup loosely packed fresh vietnamese mint leaves

Rinse noodles in strainer under hot running water. Separate noodles with fork; drain.
Heat oil in large saucepan; cook paste, stirring, until fragrant. Stir in coconut milk, stock, juice, sugar, sauce and lime leaves; bring to a boil. Reduce heat; simmer, covered, 3 minutes. Add chicken; stir until laksa is heated through.
Divide noodles among serving bowls. Ladle laksa over noodles; top with sprouts and mint, and a wedge of lime, if desired.

serves 4
per serving 28.9g fat; 2479kJ (593 cal)
tip You can substitute your favourite kind of noodle for the egg noodles.

chicken noodle soup

You can substitute rice noodles or wheat noodles
for the rice vermicelli in this recipe.

2 teaspoons olive oil
1 medium leek (350g), chopped coarsely
1 large carrot (180g), chopped coarsely
2 trimmed sticks celery (100g), chopped coarsely
1 clove garlic, crushed
1.5 litres (6 cups) chicken stock
2 cups (320g) shredded cooked chicken
50g rice vermicelli
2 tablespoons coarsely chopped fresh
   flat-leaf parsley

Heat oil in large saucepan; cook leek, carrot,
celery and garlic, stirring, until leek is soft.
Stir in stock, bring to a boil; simmer, covered,
about 20 minutes or until vegetables are tender.
Stir in chicken and noodles; simmer, uncovered,
stirring, until noodles are tender. Stir in parsley.

serves 6
per serving 6.8g fat; 652kJ (156 cal)
tip You can make soup a day ahead and refrigerate,
but add noodles only when reheating as they absorb
liquid. Similarly, if reheating leftover soup, you may
need to add water or more stock, as some liquid
will have been absorbed by the noodles.

thai chicken and lychee salad

3 cups (480g) shredded cooked chicken
565g can lychees in syrup, drained, halved, seeded
1 small red onion (100g), sliced thinly
8 green onions, sliced thinly
2 cups (160g) bean sprouts
½ cup firmly packed fresh mint leaves
½ cup firmly packed fresh coriander leaves
dressing
1 teaspoon finely grated lime rind
1 teaspoon sambal oelek
¼ cup (60ml) lime juice
1 teaspoon sesame oil
1 tablespoon brown sugar
2 teaspoons fish sauce

Make dressing.
Combine chicken, lychees, onions, sprouts, mint and coriander in large bowl.
Drizzle dressing over salad; toss gently to combine.
dressing Combine ingredients in screw-top jar; shake well.

serves 4
per serving 10.5g fat; 1265kJ (303 cal)

chicken and lime noodle salad

Bean thread noodles or vermicelli are also known as cellophane or glass noodles.

250g bean thread noodles
1 medium carrot (120g)
1 lebanese cucumber
  (130g), halved, seeded
2 green onions,
  sliced thinly
1 medium red capsicum
  (200g), sliced thinly
3 cups (480g) shredded
  cooked chicken
½ cup loosely packed
  fresh vietnamese
  mint leaves
½ cup loosely packed
  fresh coriander leaves
3 fresh small red thai
  chillies, seeded,
  sliced thinly
2 cloves garlic, crushed
⅓ cup (80ml) lime juice
⅓ cup (80ml) peanut oil
2 tablespoons fish sauce
1 tablespoon sugar

Place noodles in large heatproof
bowl; cover with boiling water. Stand
until tender; drain.
Meanwhile, using vegetable peeler,
slice carrot and cucumber into ribbons.
Combine noodles, carrot and cucumber
in large bowl with onion, capsicum,
chicken, mint, coriander, chilli and
combined remaining ingredients;
toss gently to combine.

serves 4
per serving 23.7g fat; 1633kJ (391 cal)
tips For an even more refreshing salad,
refrigerate the drained noodles overnight
before combining with remaining ingredients.
Substitute regular mint or add extra coriander
if you can't find vietnamese mint.
serving suggestion Serve accompanied
with small bowls of extra coriander leaves
and finely sliced red thai chillies.

easy chicken caesar salad

1 large cos lettuce
50g bagel crisps
1 large avocado (320g), sliced thickly
2 cups (320g) shredded cooked chicken
½ cup (40g) parmesan cheese flakes
dressing
1 large anchovy fillet, chopped finely
1 tablespoon lemon juice
¾ cup (170g) whole egg mayonnaise
1 tablespoon finely grated parmesan cheese
1 tablespoon warm water
½ clove garlic, crushed

Make dressing.
Combine torn lettuce, broken bagel crisps, avocado and chicken in large bowl. Serve drizzled with dressing and sprinkled with cheese.
dressing Combine ingredients in medium bowl.

serves 4
per serving 36.6g fat; 2175kJ (520 cal)
tip The dressing can be made up to four days ahead. This salad is best made close to serving.

tangy chicken salad

You will need to purchase one small chinese cabbage for this recipe.

1 medium carrot (120g)
1 telegraph cucumber (400g)
3 cups (480g) shredded
  cooked chicken
4 cups (320g) finely shredded
  chinese cabbage
2½ cups (200g) bean sprouts
3 green onions, sliced thinly
3 small red radishes,
  sliced thinly
¼ cup (35g) roasted unsalted
  peanuts, chopped coarsely
dressing
¼ cup (60ml) fish sauce
¼ cup (60ml) lime juice
1 tablespoon rice vinegar
1 tablespoon sugar
1 tablespoon sesame oil
1 clove garlic, crushed
½ teaspoon sambal oelek

Make dressing.
Using vegetable peeler, slice carrot and cucumber into ribbons. Place carrot and cucumber in large bowl with chicken, cabbage, sprouts, onion and radish.
Drizzle salad with dressing; toss gently to combine. Top with peanuts just before serving.
dressing Combine ingredients in screw-top jar; shake until sugar dissolves.
serves 4
per serving 14.2g fat; 1108kJ (265 cal)
tip You can prepare the salad several hours ahead. Add the dressing just before serving.

chicken pasta salad with roasted capsicum, fetta and walnut

300g frilled pasta shells
270g jar char-grilled capsicum in oil
150g fetta cheese, chopped coarsely
2½ cups (425g) coarsely chopped cooked chicken
⅓ cup (35g) toasted walnuts, chopped coarsely
1 cup loosely packed fresh basil leaves
¼ cup (60ml) red wine vinegar
1 clove garlic, crushed
2 teaspoons wholegrain mustard

Cook pasta in large saucepan of boiling water, uncovered, until just tender; drain. Rinse under cold running water; drain.

Meanwhile, drain capsicum, reserving ⅓ cup of the capsicum oil; chop capsicum coarsely.

Combine capsicum and pasta in large bowl with cheese, chicken, walnuts and basil.

Combine reserved oil with vinegar, garlic and mustard in screw-top jar; shake well. Drizzle dressing over chicken mixture; toss gently to combine.

serves 4
per serving 29.1g fat; 3251kJ (778 cal)
tips Goat cheese or any soft, crumbly cheese can be used instead of the fetta. Toasted pecan halves make a nice change from walnuts.

chicken and asparagus pasta salad

500g macaroni
250g asparagus, chopped coarsely
3 cups (480g) shredded cooked chicken
200g button mushrooms, sliced
⅓ cup chopped fresh chives
⅓ cup (80g) light sour cream
½ cup (150g) whole egg mayonnaise
1 tablespoon lemon juice
1 tablespoon wholegrain mustard

Cook pasta in large saucepan of boiling water, uncovered, until just tender; drain.
Meanwhile, boil, steam or microwave asparagus until just tender; drain.
Combine pasta, asparagus, chicken, mushrooms and chives in large bowl.
Combine sour cream, mayonnaise, juice and mustard in small bowl or jug. Add to pasta mixture, toss gently.

serves 4
per serving 44.5g fat; 3967kJ (949 cal)
tip Add the mayonnaise mixture to the pasta mixture close to serving.

chicken salad with sesame dressing

1 large barbecued chicken (900g)
2 medium carrots (240g)
½ small chinese cabbage (400g), shredded thickly
6 green onions, sliced thickly
1 cup (80g) bean sprouts
¼ cup firmly packed fresh coriander leaves
sesame dressing
2 cloves garlic, crushed
½ teaspoon sesame oil
2 tablespoons peanut oil
1 tablespoon soy sauce
1 tablespoon lemon juice
1 teaspoon sugar
1 tablespoon white wine vinegar

Cut chicken into 8 pieces.
Using a vegetable peeler, peel thin strips
lengthways from carrots. Combine carrot,
cabbage, onion, sprouts and coriander;
top with chicken.
Drizzle salad and chicken with
sesame dressing.
sesame dressing Combine ingredients
in screw-top jar; shake well.

serves 4
per serving 19.6g fat; 1419kJ (339 cal)
tip The dressing can be made a day ahead.
This recipe is best made close to serving.

chicken pasta salad

This salad is a popular choice for a hot summer
evening; it can be served warm or cold.

200g pasta shells
2½ cups (425g) chopped cooked chicken
250g cherry tomatoes, halved
1 small red capsicum (150g), chopped coarsely
6 green onions, sliced thickly
½ cup kalamata olives (80g), seeded
400g can artichoke hearts, drained, halved
¼ cup shredded fresh basil leaves
dressing
⅓ cup (80ml) lemon juice
1 tablespoon olive oil
1 tablespoon red wine vinegar
1 teaspoon sugar
2 teaspoons wholegrain mustard

Make dressing.
Cook pasta in large saucepan of boiling water,
uncovered, until just tender; drain. Rinse under
cold running water; drain.
Combine pasta with chicken, tomato, capsicum,
onion, olives, artichoke and basil in large bowl.
Drizzle dressing over salad; toss gently.
dressing Combine ingredients in screw-top
jar; shake well.

serves 4
per serve 13.9g fat; 1866kJ (446 cal)
serving suggestion Serve with crusty bread
and a green salad.
tip Use your favourite pasta shape for this salad,
or use rice instead.

creamy pesto chicken with gnocchi

Gnocchi, small Italian "dumplings" usually made from mashed potato or semolina, can be boiled, baked or fried.

500g fresh gnocchi
1 tablespoon olive oil
2 cloves garlic, crushed
½ cup (125ml) dry white wine
¼ cup (60g) basil pesto
300ml cream
2½ cups (425g) coarsely chopped cooked chicken
2 tablespoons fresh basil leaves

Cook gnocchi in large saucepan of boiling water, uncovered, about 5 minutes or until gnocchi rise to the surface and are just tender; drain.
Meanwhile, heat oil in large saucepan; cook garlic, stirring, until fragrant. Add wine, pesto and cream; bring to a boil. Reduce heat; simmer, uncovered, 3 minutes.
Add chicken and gnocchi; stir until heated through. Top with fresh basil to serve.

serves 4
per serving 46.6g fat; 2964kJ (709 cal)
tip This recipe is best made close to serving time.

chicken enchiladas with corn salsa

1 large red onion (300g),
  chopped finely
2 tablespoons
  vegetable oil
2 cloves garlic, crushed
1 tablespoon tomato paste
¼ cup (45g) drained
  bottled jalapeño chillies,
  chopped coarsely
400g can crushed
  tomatoes
1 cup (250ml)
  chicken stock
2½ cups (425g)
  coarsely chopped
  cooked chicken
10 large corn tortillas
2 cups (250g) coarsely
  grated cheddar cheese
½ cup (120g) sour cream
corn salsa
1 small red capsicum
  (150g), chopped finely
310g can corn
  kernels, drained
1 tablespoon lime juice
⅔ cup coarsely chopped
  fresh coriander

Preheat oven to moderate.
Reserve a quarter of the onion for
the corn salsa.
Heat oil in large frying pan; cook remaining
onion with garlic, stirring, until onion softens.
Add tomato paste, chilli, undrained crushed
tomatoes, stock and chicken; bring to a boil.
Reduce heat; simmer, uncovered, 5 minutes.
Using a slotted spoon, remove chicken
from pan; cover to keep warm.
Soften tortillas in oven or microwave oven,
according to manufacturer's instructions.
Dip tortillas, one at a time, in tomato mixture
in pan; place on board. Divide chicken and
half of the cheese among tortillas, placing
along edge; roll tortillas to enclose filling.
Place enchiladas, seam-side down, in large
oiled 3-litre (12 cup) shallow ovenproof
dish; enchiladas should fit snugly, without
overcrowding. Pour remaining tomato
mixture over enchiladas; top with sour cream,
sprinkle with remaining cheese.
Bake, uncovered, in moderate oven about
15 minutes or until heated through. Divide
enchiladas among serving plates; serve
with corn salsa.
corn salsa Place reserved onion in small
bowl with capsicum, corn, juice and
coriander; toss to combine.

serves 4
per serving 53.7g fat; 3854kJ (922 cal)

tagliatelle, chicken and peas in mustard cream sauce

250g tagliatelle
1 tablespoon olive oil
1 medium brown onion (150g), chopped finely
2 cloves garlic, crushed
½ cup (125ml) dry white wine
1 tablespoon dijon mustard
1 cup (250ml) cream
2 cups (250g) frozen peas, thawed
2 cups (320g) shredded cooked chicken
¼ cup finely chopped fresh garlic chives

Cook pasta in large saucepan of boiling water, uncovered, until just tender; drain.

Meanwhile, heat oil in large saucepan; cook onion and garlic, stirring, until onion softens. Add wine and mustard; bring to a boil. Reduce heat; simmer, uncovered, 5 minutes. Stir in cream; return mixture to a boil, then simmer again, uncovered, about 5 minutes or until sauce thickens slightly.

Stir in drained peas and chicken; stir over low heat until mixture is hot.

Place pasta and chives in pan with chicken and pea sauce; toss gently to combine.

serves 4
per serving 35.1g fat; 2861kJ (684 cal)

lemon ginger chicken

2 cups (400g) long-grain white rice
2 teaspoons olive oil
4cm piece fresh ginger (20g), grated finely
2 tablespoons honey
2 teaspoons cornflour
½ cup (125ml) water
¼ cup (60ml) lemon juice
1 tablespoon light soy sauce
1 tablespoon sweet chilli sauce
1 large barbecued chicken (900g), quartered

Cook rice in large saucepan of boiling water, uncovered, until just tender; drain.

Meanwhile, heat oil in large frying pan; cook ginger and honey, stirring, 1 minute. Blend cornflour with the water in small jug; stir into pan with juice and sauces. Cook, stirring, until mixture boils and thickens.

Add chicken; reduce heat. Simmer, uncovered, 5 minutes, turning chicken once during cooking. Serve chicken with rice, and a wedge of lemon, if desired.

serves 4
per serving 22.5g fat; 3002kJ (718 cal)

chicken with cacciatore-style sauce

1 tablespoon olive oil
1 medium brown onion (150g), chopped finely
2 cloves garlic, crushed
1 tablespoon tomato paste
2 x 400g cans tomatoes
½ cup (125ml) dry red wine
2 bay leaves
4 anchovy fillets, drained, chopped finely
1 cup (120g) seeded kalamata olives
2 tablespoons fresh oregano leaves
1 large barbecued chicken (900g), quartered, skinned

Heat oil in large saucepan; cook onion and garlic, stirring, until onion softens. Add paste, undrained crushed tomatoes, wine, bay leaves, anchovy and olives; bring to a boil. Reduce heat; simmer, uncovered, 4 minutes.
Discard bay leaves; stir oregano through sauce.
Add chicken to sauce; stir until heated through.

serves 4
per serving 16.1g fat; 1637kJ (392 cal)
serving suggestion Serve with a bowl of freshly cooked short pasta, such as farfalle or penne.

chicken with creamy sun-dried tomato sauce

1 tablespoon olive oil
1 medium brown onion (150g), chopped finely
2 teaspoons tomato paste
⅔ cup (100g) drained sun-dried tomatoes,
   chopped coarsely
¼ cup (60ml) dry white wine
½ cup (125ml) chicken stock
300ml cream
2 tablespoons coarsely chopped fresh sage
1 large barbecued chicken (900g), skinned, quartered

Heat oil in large frying pan; cook onion, stirring,
until onion is lightly browned.
Add paste, tomato and wine; cook, uncovered,
until liquid is almost evaporated. Add stock,
cream and sage; bring to a boil.
Add chicken; reduce heat. Simmer, uncovered,
until sauce thickens slightly and chicken is
heated through.

serves 4
per serving 44.7g fat; 2638kJ (631 cal)
tip The sage can be substituted with any
other fresh herb.
serving suggestion Serve with steamed white rice.

fried rice

You will need to cook about 1⅔ cups rice for this recipe.

5 cups cooked long-grain white rice
2 teaspoons vegetable oil
2 eggs, beaten lightly
1 cup (125g) frozen peas
1 cup (160g) frozen corn kernels
2½ cups (425g) coarsely chopped cooked chicken
6 green onions, chopped coarsely
¼ cup (60ml) soy sauce
2 tablespoons coarsely chopped fresh
   flat-leaf parsley
⅓ cup (80ml) sweet chilli sauce

Spread rice over shallow tray and refrigerate, uncovered, several hours or overnight. (This will keep the rice grains separate, preventing stickiness.)
Heat a teaspoon of the oil in large heated wok or frying pan, add egg and swirl the wok so egg forms a thin omelette; cook until set. Transfer omelette to board and cut into strips.
Heat remaining oil in wok, add peas and corn and stir-fry until hot. Add chicken and stir-fry until hot. Add rice, onion, soy sauce and parsley; stir-fry until hot.
Serve fried rice topped with omelette and sweet chilli sauce.

serves 6
per serving 10.1g fat; 1641kJ (393 cal)

baked pasta
and chicken carbonara

250g spaghetti
1 tablespoon olive oil
500g button mushrooms, quartered
2 cloves garlic, crushed
1 teaspoon coarsely chopped fresh thyme
¼ cup (60ml) dry white wine
¾ cup (180ml) chicken stock
425g jar carbonara sauce
3 green onions, sliced thickly
3 cups (480g) shredded cooked chicken
⅔ cup (50g) finely grated parmesan cheese
⅓ cup (25g) stale breadcrumbs

Cook pasta in large saucepan of boiling water, uncovered, until just tender; drain. Rinse under cold running water; drain.

Meanwhile, preheat oven to very hot. Heat oil in large frying pan; cook mushrooms, garlic and thyme, stirring, until mushrooms are lightly browned. Add wine and stock; bring to a boil. Cook, stirring, about 5 minutes or until liquid is reduced by half; remove from heat.

Add pasta to mushroom mixture with sauce, onion, chicken and half of the cheese; toss gently to combine.

Combine remaining cheese and breadcrumbs in small bowl. Pour pasta mixture into lightly greased 3-litre (12 cup) baking dish; sprinkle top with breadcrumb mixture. Bake, uncovered, in very hot oven about 10 minutes or until top is lightly browned.

serves 4
per serving 25.7g fat; 4046kJ (968 cal)

moroccan chicken with couscous

1 cup (250ml) vegetable stock
1½ cups (300g) couscous
1 medium red onion (170g), sliced thinly
3 cups (480g) shredded cooked chicken
½ cup (75g) coarsely chopped dried apricots
½ cup (80g) sultanas
¼ cup finely chopped fresh mint
1 tablespoon pine nuts
2 teaspoons cumin seeds
¾ cup (180ml) bottled fat-free french dressing

Bring stock to a boil in large saucepan; remove
from heat. Stir in couscous. Cover; stand about
5 minutes or until stock is absorbed, fluffing with fork.
Stir in onion, chicken, apricot, sultanas and mint.
Meanwhile, stir pine nuts and seeds in small
frying pan over low heat until just fragrant. Add to
couscous with dressing; toss gently to combine.

serves 4
per serving 12.6g fat; 2745kJ (657 cal)

chicken and vegie pie

*We used chilled fillo pastry sheets, available
in 375g packets from the refrigerated section
of the supermarket.*

60g butter
1 medium leek (350g), sliced thinly
⅓ cup (50g) plain flour
¾ cup (180ml) milk
1 cup (250ml) chicken stock
3 cups (480g) shredded cooked chicken
2½ cups (350g) frozen peas, corn and capsicum mix
¼ cup coarsely chopped fresh flat-leaf parsley
4 sheets fillo pastry
cooking-oil spray

Preheat oven to hot.
Melt butter in large saucepan; cook leek, stirring,
until softened. Add flour; cook, stirring, until mixture
bubbles and thickens.
Gradually stir in milk and stock; heat, stirring,
until mixture boils and thickens. Add chicken,
vegetables and parsley; stir until heated through.
Spoon chicken pie filling into shallow
1.5-litre (6 cup) ovenproof dish.
Place one sheet of pastry over filling; spray
with cooking-oil spray. Repeat process with
remaining pastry, overlapping pastry around dish.
Roll and fold pastry around edge of dish. Spray
top of pastry with cooking-oil spray. Bake,
uncovered, in hot oven 10 minutes.

serves 4
per serving 25.3g fat; 2124kJ (508 cal)
tip The pie filling can be made a day ahead.

glossary

barbecue sauce a spicy sauce used to marinate, baste or as a condiment.

basil we used sweet basil unless otherwise specified.

bay leaves aromatic leaves from the bay tree used to flavour soups and stews.

bean sprouts also known as bean shoots; tender growths of assorted beans and seeds germinated for consumption as sprouts. The most common are mung bean, soy bean, alfalfa and snow pea sprouts.

breadcrumbs, stale one- or two-day-old bread made into crumbs by grating, blending or processing.

butter use salted or unsalted (sweet) butter; 125g is equal to one stick of butter.

capsicum also known as bell pepper or, simply, pepper. They can be red, green, yellow, orange or purplish black. Discard seeds and membranes before use.

cheese
cheddar: the most common cow-milk "tasty" cheese; should be aged, hard and have a pronounced bite.
fetta: Greek in origin; crumbly textured goat- or sheep-milk cheese with sharp, salty taste.
parmesan: also known as parmigiano; hard, grainy cow-milk cheese which originated in the Parma region of Italy.
pizza: commercial blend of processed, grated mozzarella, cheddar and parmesan.

chilli
jalapeño: fairly hot green chillies, available bottled in brine, or fresh from specialty greengrocers.

small red thai: small, bright red and medium-hot in flavour.
sweet chilli sauce: made from red chillies, sugar, garlic and vinegar; used as a condiment more often than in cooking.

chinese cabbage also known as peking or napa cabbage, wong bok or petsai. Elongated shape with pale, crinkly leaves.

coconut milk second pressing (less rich) from grated mature coconut flesh; available in light or low-fat version.

coriander also known as pak chee, cilantro or chinese parsley; leafy, bright-green herb with a pungent flavour.

corn chips packaged snack food; fried corn tortilla pieces.

cornflour also known as cornstarch; used as a thickening agent in cooking.

cos lettuce also known as romaine lettuce.

couscous fine, grain-like cereal product, made from semolina.

creamed corn available in cans in most supermarkets.

cumin seeds also known as zeera.

egg some recipes in this book may call for raw or barely cooked eggs; exercise caution if there is a salmonella problem in your area.

fillo pastry also known as phyllo dough; comes in tissue-thin pastry sheets bought chilled or frozen.

fish sauce also known as naam pla or nuoc naam. Made from pulverised, salted fermented fish; has a pungent smell and strong taste. Use according to taste.

flour, plain an all-purpose flour, made from wheat.

ginger also known as green or root ginger; the thick gnarled root of a tropical plant.

iceberg lettuce heavy, round lettuce with tightly packed leaves and crisp texture.

kaffir lime leaves also known as bai magrood; two glossy dark-green leaves joined end to end. Sold fresh, dried or frozen; dried leaves are less potent so double the quantity if using in place of fresh leaves.

kalamata olive small, sharp-tasting, brine-cured black olive.

lavash flat, unleavened bread of Mediterranean origin.

lebanese cucumber long, slender and thin-skinned; also known as the European or burpless cucumber.

lychees sweet-flavoured fruit; peel away skin, remove seed and use. Available in cans.

mayonnaise we use whole egg mayonnaise in our recipes.

mexican-style beans canned mixture of kidney or pinto beans cooked with tomato, peppers, onion, garlic and various spices.

mint, vietnamese not mint at all, but a pungent, peppery narrow-leafed member of the buckwheat family. Also known as cambodian mint, pak pai, rau ram and laksa leaf.

mushrooms
button: small, cultivated white mushrooms with mild flavour.
shiitake: when fresh, are also known as chinese black, forest or golden oak mushrooms. Large cultivated mushroom with earthy flavour. When dried, they are known as donko or dried chinese mushrooms; rehydrate before use.

mustard

dijon: pale brown, distinctively flavoured, mild French mustard.

wholegrain: also known as seeded. French-style coarse-grain mustard made from crushed mustard seeds and dijon-style French mustard.

noodles

bean thread: also known as wun sen or cellophane or glass noodles because they are transparent when cooked; made from extruded mung bean paste. White in colour, very delicate and fine; available dried in bundles.

fresh egg: also known as ba mee or yellow noodles; made from wheat flour and eggs, and sold fresh or dried. Range in size from very fine strands to wide, spaghetti-like pieces.

rice vermicelli: also known as sen mee, mei fun or bee hoon. Similar to bean threads, only longer and made with rice flour.

oil

cooking oil spray: we use a cholesterol-free cooking spray made from canola oil.

olive: made from ripe olives. Extra virgin and virgin are the first and second pressings, respectively, of the olives, and therefore considered the best. Extra light or light refers to taste not fat levels.

peanut: pressed from ground peanuts; most commonly used oil in Asian cooking because of its high smoke point (handles high heat without burning).

sesame: made from roasted, crushed, white sesame seeds; used as a flavouring.

vegetable: oils sourced from plants rather than animal fats.

onion

green: also known as scallion or (incorrectly) shallot; immature onion picked before the bulb has formed, having a long, bright-green edible stalk.

red: also known as spanish, red spanish or bermuda onion; sweet, large, purple-red onion.

parsley, flat-leaf also known as continental or italian parsley.

pine nuts also known as pignoli; small, cream-coloured kernels from pine cones.

refried beans pinto beans, cooked twice – soaked and boiled, then mashed and fried, traditionally in lard. Available canned in supermarkets.

rice paper rounds made from rice paste and stamped into rounds; dipped momentarily in water they become pliable wrappers for food.

rice, long-grain white elongated grain, remains separate when cooked; most popular steaming rice in Asia.

sambal oelek also ulek or olek; a salty paste made from ground chillies and vinegar.

snow pea tendrils the growing shoots of the plant; sold by greengrocers.

stock 1 cup (250ml) stock is the equivalent of 1 cup (250ml) water plus 1 crumbled stock cube (or 1 teaspoon stock powder). If you prefer, use fresh homemade stock.

sugar we used coarse granulated table sugar, also known as crystal sugar, unless otherwise specified.

brown: an extremely soft, fine granulated sugar retaining molasses for its characteristic colour and flavour.

sultanas also known as raisins.

telegraph cucumber long and green with ridges running its entire length; also known as continental cucumber.

teriyaki sauce a homemade or commercially bottled sauce usually made from soy sauce, mirin, sugar, ginger and other spices; a distinctive glaze when brushed on grilled meat.

tomato

canned: whole peeled tomatoes in natural juices.

cherry: also known as Tiny Tim or Tom Thumb tomatoes, small and round.

paste: triple-concentrated tomato puree used to flavour soups, stews, sauces and casseroles.

sun-dried: we used sun-dried tomatoes packaged in oil, unless otherwise specified.

tortilla thin, round unleavened bread originating in Mexico; can be made at home or purchased frozen, fresh or vacuum-packed. Two kinds are available: one made from wheat flour and the other from corn.

vinegar

red wine: based on fermented red wine.

rice: a colourless vinegar made from fermented rice and flavoured with sugar and salt. Also known as seasoned rice vinegar. Sherry can be substituted.

white wine: made from spirit of cane sugar.

wine we used good-quality dry white and red wines in our recipes.

zucchini also known as courgette.

index

facts & figures

These conversions are approximate only, but the difference between an exact and the approximate conversion of various liquid and dry measures is minimal and will not affect your cooking results.

Note: NZ, Canada, US and UK all use 15ml tablespoons. Australian tablespoons measure 20ml. All cup and spoon measurements are level.

Measuring equipment
The difference between one country's measuring cups and another's is, at most, within a 2 or 3 teaspoon variance. (For the record, 1 Australian metric measuring cup holds approximately 250ml.) The most accurate way of measuring dry ingredients is to weigh them. For liquids, use a clear glass or plastic jug having metric markings.

How to measure
When using graduated measuring cups, shake dry ingredients loosely into the appropriate cup. Do not tap the cup on a bench or tightly pack the ingredients unless directed to do so. Level the top of measuring cups and measuring spoons with a knife. When measuring liquids, place a clear glass or plastic jug having metric markings on a flat surface to check accuracy at eye level.

Dry measures

metric	imperial
15g	½oz
30g	1oz
60g	2oz
90g	3oz
125g	4oz (¼lb)
155g	5oz
185g	6oz
220g	7oz
250g	8oz (½lb)
280g	9oz
315g	10oz
345g	11oz
375g	12oz (¾lb)
410g	13oz
440g	14oz
470g	15oz
500g	16oz (1lb)
750g	24oz (1½lb)
1kg	32oz (2lb)

Liquid measures

metric	imperial
30 ml	1 fluid oz
60 ml	2 fluid oz
100 ml	3 fluid oz
125 ml	4 fluid oz
150 ml	5 fluid oz (¼ pint/1 gill)
190 ml	6 fluid oz
250 ml (1cup)	8 fluid oz
300 ml	10 fluid oz (½ pint)
500 ml	16 fluid oz
600 ml	20 fluid oz (1 pint)
1000 ml (1litre)	1¾ pints

Helpful measures

metric	imperial
3mm	⅛in
6mm	¼in
1cm	½in
2cm	¾in
2.5cm	1in
6cm	2½in
8cm	3in
20cm	8in
23cm	9in
25cm	10in
30cm	12in (1ft)

Oven temperatures
These oven temperatures are only a guide. Always check the manufacturer's manual.

	°C (Celsius)	°F (Fahrenheit)	Gas Mark
Very slow	120	250	½
Slow	140 – 150	275 – 300	1 – 2
Moderately slow	170	325	3
Moderate	180 –190	350 – 375	4 – 5
Moderately hot	200	400	6
Hot	220 – 230	425 – 450	7 – 8
Very hot	240	475	9

We use large eggs with an average weight of 60g.

at your fingertips

These elegant slipcovers store up to 12 mini books and make the books instantly accessible.

And the metric measuring cups and spoons make following our recipes a piece of cake.

Book Holder
Australia and overseas:
$8.95 (incl. GST).

Metric Measuring Set
Australia: $6.50 (incl. GST).
New Zealand: $A8.00.
Elsewhere: $A9.95.
Prices include postage and handling. This offer is available in all countries.

Mail or fax Photocopy and complete the coupon below and post to ACP Books Reader Offer, ACP Books, GPO Box 4967, Sydney NSW 2001, or fax to (02) 9267 4967.

Phone Have your credit card details ready, then phone 136 116 (Mon-Fri, 8.00am-6.00pm; Sat, 8.00am-6.00pm).

Australian residents We accept the credit cards listed on the coupon, money orders and cheques.

Overseas residents We accept the credit cards listed on the coupon, drafts in $A drawn on an Australian bank, and also UK, NZ and US cheques in the currency of the country of issue. Credit card charges are at the exchange rate current at the time of payment.

Photocopy and complete coupon below

☐ **Book Holder** ☐ **Metric Measuring Set**

Please indicate number(s) required.

Mr/Mrs/Ms _____

Address _____

_____

Postcode _____ Country _____

Ph: Business hours ( ) _____

I enclose my cheque/money order for $ _____ payable to ACP Publishing.

OR: please charge $ _____ to my ☐ Bankcard ☐ Mastercard

☐ Visa ☐ American Express ☐ Diners Club

Expiry date ____ /____

Card number

Cardholder's signature _____

Please allow up to 30 days delivery within Australia.
Allow up to 6 weeks for overseas deliveries.
Both offers expire 31/12/05. HLMBC05

Food director Pamela Clark
Food editor Louise Patniotis
Nutritional information Laila Ibram

ACP BOOKS
Editorial director Susan Tomnay
Creative director Hieu Chi Nguyen
Senior editor Julie Collard
Designer Caryl Wiggins
Publishing manager (sales) Brian Cearnes
Publishing manager (rights & new projects)
 Jane Hazell
Sales & marketing coordinator Caroline Lowry
Marketing director Nicole Pizanis
Pre-press Harry Palmer
Production manager Carol Currie
Business manager Seymour Cohen
Business analyst Martin Howes
Chief executive officer John Alexander
Group publisher Pat Ingram
Publisher Sue Wannan
Editor-in-chief Deborah Thomas
Produced by ACP Books, Sydney.
Printing by Dai Nippon Printing in Korea.
Published by ACP Publishing Pty Limited,
54 Park St, Sydney;
GPO Box 4088, Sydney, NSW 2001.
Ph: (02) 9282 8618 Fax: (02) 9267 9438.
acpbooks@acp.com.au
www.acpbooks.com.au
To order books phone 136 116.
Send recipe enquiries to
Recipeenquiries@acp.com.au
Australia Distributed by Network Services,
GPO Box 4088, Sydney, NSW 1028.
Ph: (02) 9282 8777 Fax: (02) 9264 3278.
United Kingdom Distributed by Australian Consolidated
Press (UK), Moulton Park Business Centre, Red House
Road, Moulton Park, Northampton, NN3 6AQ.
Ph: (01604) 497 531 Fax: (01604) 497 533
acpukltd@aol.com
Canada Distributed by Whitecap Books Ltd,
351 Lynn Ave, North Vancouver, BC, V7J 2C4,
Ph: (604) 980 9852 Fax: (604) 980 8197
customerservice@whitecap.ca
www.whitecap.ca
New Zealand Distributed by Netlink Distribution
Company, ACP Media Centre, Cnr Fanshawe and
Beaumont Streets, Westhaven, Auckland.
PO Box 47906, Ponsonby, Auckland, NZ.
Ph: (9) 366 9966 ask@ndcnz.co.nz
South Africa Distributed by PSD Promotions,
30 Diesel Road, Isando, Gauteng, Johannesburg;
PO Box 1175, Isando, 1600, Gauteng, Johannesburg.
Ph: (27 11) 392 6065/7 Fax: (27 11) 392 6079/80
orders@psdprom.co.za

Clark, Pamela.
The Australian Women's Weekly Barbecue Chicken.
Includes index.
ISBN 1 86396 405 3
1. Cookery (Chicken). 2. Convenience foods.
3. Quick and easy cookery. I. Title. II. Title: Australian
Women's Weekly.
641.665
© ACP Publishing Pty Limited 2005
ABN 18 053 273 546
Cover Chicken pasta salad, page 39.
Back cover at left, Chicken nachos, page 12;
at right, Chicken and vegie pie, page 59.
Stylist Stephanie Souvlis
Photographer Georgie Cole
Home economist Elizabeth Macri